Interview Guide For Employers Of Labour: A Resource For Supervisors And Others Involved In The Selection Process

BOB REX

All rights reserved.

No portion of this book may be reproduced, distributed or transmitted in any form without written permission from the publisher or author,including photocopying, recording, or other electronic or mechanical methods, except in the brief quotation embodied in critical reviews and certain other noncommercial uses permitted by copyright law.

Copyright © 2024, by Bob Rex.

Table of contents

Introduction
Chapter 1
Chapter 2
Chapter 3

Introduction

Most employers are aware that an effective and legally sound pre-employment screening program may well increase the chances of selecting qualified, motivated, dependable employees. Although this guide cannot answer every question that might arise in the pre-employment selection context, it does provide basic guidance on applicable federal and state laws and a sound process for pre-employment screening and interviewing.

As an employer, you want to select the applicant that is the best fit for the position. Your interviewers have critical responsibilities to select employees on the basis of job-related qualifications in accordance with all applicable laws and regulations. You, the employer, must carefully define the position and the qualifications it requires. Then, the process becomes a search for the right match of applicant to position.

Well-planned pre-employment interviews and carefully written applications or resumes can help ensure that you find the person who is the best match. For a hiring process to be effective, everyone involved must be aware that significant legal limitations impact an employer's selection decisions. Whether a faculty member, human resource professional, office manager, or first-line supervisor, the interviewer must know which information is fair game, which is not, and how to avoid unnecessary liability.

This guide is designed to provide an overview of key employment-related legislation with specific emphasis on the do's and don'ts in order to decrease the likelihood of mistakes that result in adverse legal action against the institution. The guide also includes pre-employment selection process suggestions and several applications to help managers with various parts of the selection process.

It is recommended that the hiring manager uses a structured interview process. What is a Structured Interview? Structured interviews are interviews that use multiple mechanisms (or elements) to help make the interview job-related and systematic. Research shows that structured interviews are twice as effective as unstructured interviews in predicting job performance. Unstructured interviews, where interviewers rely on unaided judgment, are subject to bias and may expose you to future complaints or challenges. The elements of a structured interview include:

1. Base questions on job analysis. (Ensures fairness and impartiality)

2. Ask effective questions. (Evokes responses that help you make the decision)

3. Ask each candidate the same questions. (Ensures fairness and impartiality)

4. Use detailed rating scales. (Helps quantify subjective data)

5. Train interviewers. (Ensures professionalism)

6. Use interview panels so that more than one person conducts the interview. (Provides checks and balances to ensure fairness and impartiality)

7. Take notes. (Memory can be short and provides paper trail for defending selection if needed)

8. Assess candidate responses objectively by using the rating scales to score candidates. (Promotes objectivity and complies with Merit System Principles)

Chapter 1

How To Interview Candidates: Preparation & Interviewing Tips

The hour or two you spend interviewing a candidate for any position within your organization is critical to both the organization and to your career. It is important for the growth and health of the organization in that a great hire can add immeasurably to the bottom line. For you, the manager/owner/president, it is important for you to hire the best fit, both culturally and skill set.

A key element in conducting a professional interview that will allow you to hire only the best will depend on what you do before the interview actually occurs. An agenda should be prepared for this meeting. Most of the time the candidate comes to the interview prepared. They usually arrive with a list of questions and several well thought-out statements regarding their past achievements. The interviewer is strongly recommended to match the candidate's efforts by spending time preparing for this meeting.

A list of questions should be formulated that key into an exploration of the following personal traits: attitude, motivation, initiative, stability, planning, insight, and social skills. If the interviewer plans to interview more than one candidate, then some sort of rating system should be devised (ranked 1-2-3) that will allow for objectivity. Secondly, the interviewer should be prepared to sell both the opportunity and the company. Remember, good candidates are at a premium and if they are interviewing with you, they're probably interviewing with your competition. Be prepared to list the reasons for joining your company. Why should the candidate resign his/her current position to work for you?

Interviewing has been called an art, and there's no doubt that it calls for insight and creativity. But it's also a science, requiring process, methods, and consistency to produce truly accurate and effective results. Look at it this way: Your art will flourish within the sound framework of a systematic, scientific approach.

Define your objectives before you start
Even if you think you're an expert interviewer, a "seat-of-the-pants" approach can backfire. Take the time to clearly define what you are looking for before you begin recruiting.

- Describe the position's duties and the technical knowledge and skills required to do the job.

- Identify success factors: How did previous top performers in this job behave?
- Establish performance expectations: What do you expect this person to accomplish?

For this step, bring in the hiring manager as well as peers or those who have performed the job in the past to make sure that you are painting an accurate picture of the ideal candidate. Armed with this information, you'll be better able to evaluate each candidate.

Select your questions in advance

Don't rely on a job description and a candidate's resume to structure the interview. You'll get much better information if you carefully pre-select questions that allow you to evaluate whether a candidate has those skills and behaviors you've identified as essential for the job.

You might include some or all of these types of questions:

1. Icebreakers: As their name implies, icebreakers are used to build rapport and set candidates at ease before beginning the formal interview. Examples:
- Did you have any trouble finding our office?
- Before we start, would you like a cup of coffee or a glass of ice water?

2. Traditional Questions: With these, you can gather general information about a candidate and their skills and experience.
Because these questions are asked often, many candidates will have prepared answers to them, so they can be used to help candidates feel at ease in the early stages of an interview. Examples:

- What are your greatest strengths?
- What is your experience with [competency, skill, function, etc.]?

- Why do you want to work for us?

3. Situational Questions: Ask candidates what they would do in a specific situation relevant to the job at hand. These questions can help you understand a candidate's thought process. Examples:

- How would you deal with an irate customer?
- If we were to hire you, what is the first thing you would do?
- How do you deal with stress on the job?

4. Behavior-Based Questions: These require candidates to share a specific example from their past experience. Each a complete answer from a candidate should be in the form of a SAR response—the complete Situation, Action, and Result. If a candidate skips any of these three elements, prompt them to fill in the blanks. Examples:

- Tell me about a crisis you could have prevented. Did you do anything differently after the crisis had passed?
- Tell me how you resolve crises by deploying your team members. Give me a specific example.
- Crises usually require us to act quickly. In retrospect, how would you have handled a recent crisis differently, if you had been given more time to think before acting?

5. Culture-Fit Questions: These will help you select candidates who are motivated and suited to perform well in the unique environment of your organization. Examples:

- What gave you the greatest feeling of achievement in your last job? Why was this so satisfying?
- Why did you choose this type of work?
- What motivates you to work hard? Give me some examples.

Build an interview team

Whenever possible, have more than one person interview candidates; you'll gain a balanced perspective and be more likely to have a fair hiring process. In addition to the reporting manager and a Human Resources representative, think about including some of the people who will be working with the new hire.

Chapter 2

How To Interview Candidates: The Interview Process & Beyond

Before the Interview

- Put candidates at ease: Interviewing can be stressful, so do your best to help candidates relax. Make sure each candidate is greeted and escorted, if necessary, to the interview location. Start with low-key questions.

- Don't judge on first impressions: We've all met them-- people who don't make a great first impression but end up being great employees. To make sure you don't overlook these diamonds in the rough, withhold judgment until you've had the chance to thoroughly evaluate a candidate's capabilities and potential.

During the Interview

- Tell the candidate a little about the job: While you don't want to dominate the interview time, you should start with a brief summary of the position, including the prime responsibilities, reporting structure, key challenges, and performance criteria. This will help the candidate provide relevant examples and responses.

- Don't be afraid to improvise: Plan your questions, but don't feel you must ask only those you've chosen in advance. "Be responsive to what the candidate tells you, and build new questions off their answers," says

Shelly Goldman, executive recruiter with The Goldman Group Advantage, an executive recruiting firm in Reston, Virginia.

- Listen: If you are doing most of the talking during an interview, you will not be able to obtain enough information to distinguish between candidates or to determine a candidate's true competencies. A general guideline is to spend 80 percent of your time listening and only 20 percent talking.

- Take notes: While you won't want to transcribe everything the candidate says, do write down important points, key accomplishments, good examples, and other information that will help you remember and fairly evaluate each candidate. An interview guide, prepared in advance, will make note-taking easier and give you a structure for capturing key information.

- Invite candidates to ask questions: This can be the most valuable part of the interview. Why do they want to be here-- is it the challenge of the job, advances in the industry, or something specific about your company? Or is the candidate fixated on salary, benefits, and time off? If the candidate has no questions this should be a red flag, especially for senior-level employees. Make a note of what the candidate asks, and be sure to follow up if you can't provide the answer immediately.

- Follow legal interviewing guidelines: It is critically important that every interviewer at your company, from HR clerks to top executives, understand and follow legal hiring guidelines. The easiest way to keep your interviews fully compliant is to ask only questions that relate to the job, eliminating the potential for bias by not introducing questions or scenarios that will elicit irrelevant information.

After the Interview

- Let candidates know what they can expect: A pet peeve of many job seekers is that they are left "hanging" after an interview, or they are promised follow-up that never comes. If the candidate is a good fit, be clear about what the next steps will be. And if the candidate is not a good fit? "Always end the interview on a positive note, but be genuine," says Goldman. "Don't tell the candidate to call you if you don't mean it."

- Compare notes and reach consensus: The post-interview evaluation is the time to compare notes and advance the hiring decision. Each interviewer should be prepared to back up remarks and recommendations with specific examples and notes from the interview.

- Deepen the questions as you narrow the field: Subsequent interviews with finalists are valuable opportunities to learn more about them. Consider adding "show me" exercises such as a strategic planning exercise or a "walk me through what you'd do" activity involving a real business challenge the individual would be facing.
- Your search consultant will be in contact with you once they have debriefed the candidate. Be prepared to give your honest feedback to your consultant. Decide if they are a fit or not.

Create a Positive Image for Your Organization

Your interview process reflects the value your company places on each candidate and, by extension, each employee. Be a good ambassador for your company by conducting a professional interview, communicating honestly, and basing hiring decisions on an honest evaluation of each candidate's capabilities. Not only will you make great hires, but you'll build goodwill in the community and enhance your future recruiting efforts.

Chapter 3

How To Interview Candidates: Legal Interview Questions & Hiring Guidelines

UNIFORM GUIDELINES ON EMPLOYEE SELECTION PROCEDURES

In 1978, the Equal Employment Opportunity Commission (EEOC) developed a uniform set of guidelines for employers to follow when using pre-employment testing or other selection procedures as a basis for any employment decision. These guidelines apply to all selection criteria, including educational degree requirements, job experience and skills tests. Under the guidelines, employers may not use selection criteria that have a disparate impact on applicants in protected classes unless the criteria have been "validated." An employment practice has a disparate impact if it has a significant adverse impact on a protected group.

The employer must make every effort to ensure that all employment selection tools, such as interviews, application forms, resumes, vitae and skills/abilities assessments directly relate to successful performance of the job. For example, employers might prefer applicants with a high school diploma or a college degree, related job experience and high scores on skill-based assessments.

However, if these desired qualifications disproportionately screen out applicants in protected classes, they may be discriminatory. Similarly, subjective procedures may discriminate if they adversely affect a protected class of applicants. The employer may have to prove that such selection procedures are related to the job. Usually, such proof is difficult to produce because procedures must be validated in the same manner as professionally developed assessments.

When alternatives to selection criteria exist, employers are under an affirmative duty to investigate those that have an adverse impact, even if they are valid according to EEOC guidelines. If two or more alternatives that serve the employer's legitimate interest exist, the employer should use the selection criterion with the least adverse impact.

Employers cannot use pre-hire inquiries or qualifying factors that disproportionately screen out applicants in protected classes if the inquiries or factors are invalid predictors of successful job performance or unjustified by "business necessity." When employers devise or review application forms or seek information from job applicants, they should determine:

(1) Will the answers to this question, if used in making a selection, have a disparate effect in screening out applicants in protected classes? and

(2) Is this information essential to judge an applicant's qualifications for the job in question?

An employer should be able to demonstrate through statistical evidence that any selection procedure that has a disparate impact on groups protected by law is related to the job. If the employer cannot establish this claim or does not perform a technical validation study, he or she should discontinue or alter the procedure to eliminate the discriminatory effect. Even when a selection procedure with an adverse impact can be validated, an employer may not use it if other procedures would accomplish the same goal with less discriminatory effect.

STATE AND FEDERAL LAWS AND REGULATIONS GOVERNING EMPLOYMENT PRACTICES

In addition to the EEOC guidelines, many state and federal laws and regulations govern employment practices and affect the hiring process. The major federal laws that apply to most employers include:

• Title VII of the Civil Rights Act of 1964 - Title VII prohibits employment discrimination based on specifically enumerated categories. Pre-employment inquiries concerning race, color, religion, sex or national origin might constitute evidence of discrimination prohibited by Title VII. Inquiries that either directly or indirectly result in the disclosure of such information, unless otherwise explained, might be a Title VII violation.

• Equal Pay Act - The Equal Pay Act bars wage differentials based on sex.

- Age Discrimination in Employment Act - The Age Discrimination in Employment Act bars age-based employment practices that discriminate against people 40 years of age or older, subject to certain exceptions.
- Vocational Rehabilitation Act - The Vocational Rehabilitation Act bars discrimination against individuals with disabilities.
- Pregnancy Discrimination Act- The Pregnancy Discrimination Act bars discrimination against pregnant applicants and employees.
- Civil Rights Act of 1991 - The Civil Rights Act of 1991 provides remedies and protections, in addition to those previously available under Title VII, to applicants, employees and former employees who contend that they are victims of employment discrimination.
- Immigration Reform and Control Act - The Immigration Reform and Control Act makes it unlawful for employers to knowingly hire illegal aliens and mandates

detailed record-keeping procedures for any employees hired, including U.S. citizens, regardless of the size of the employer or of the position involved.

- Americans with Disabilities Act - The Americans with Disabilities Act prohibits discrimination against qualified individuals with disabilities and requires reasonable accommodation for disabled applicants and employees who are capable of performing the essential functions of a position.

In addition, federal government contractors may be subject to Executive Order 11246, Section 503 of the Vocational Rehabilitation Act, and the Vietnam Era Readjustment Act, all of which require affirmative action in employment practices.

Additional state laws, regulations, guidelines, and local ordinances might apply to employment practices. Most states have fair employment or human rights commissions to interpret and enforce provisions of state law barring employment discrimination. Some state agencies have stricter rules than federal agencies. Employers must be familiar with all local laws and regulations pertaining to employment and hiring (for example, city ordinances banning discrimination based on the sexual orientation of applicants).

In reviewing and revising employment applications, resumes, vitae and other pre-employment inquiries, employers should closely examine applicable local, state and federal employment inquiry guidelines and consult legal counsel to ensure that the pre-selection process is in full compliance with the law.

Fair hiring laws were enacted to give every candidate a fair shake in the interview and selection process. Yet more than 40 years after the first of these guidelines became law, job candidates today still are asked questions that are illegal, insulting, and irrelevant to job performance. The keys to eradicating this kind of behavior are ongoing education and consistent interviewing and selection practices.

Job Relevance is the Key Factor

Your interview questions should be designed to determine a candidate's capability to perform the essential functions you have defined for the job. Just be sure to couch your inquiries in job-relevant language, and don't make assumptions about a candidate's ability or disability.

For example, let's say you are interviewing a wheelchair-bound candidate for an account manager position, and you have determined that an essential function of the job is to visit client sites. It's perfectly legal to ask how the candidate would perform this essential function:

"This job will require you to be out of the office meeting with clients several days per week. Can you tell me how you would get around?"

It is not OK to say to this same candidate, "How long have you been disabled?"

In other areas, where a disability is not visible, again you should confine your questions to essential job functions or workplace environment issues. For example, while you cannot ask a candidate if he or she has children or has adequate child care, you can ask about ability to perform the job:
"This job requires you to travel overnight about 2 days per week and to attend out-of-town conferences once per month. Does this travel schedule prevent a problem for you?"

Legal and Illegal Inquiries

Following are some of the key areas that are covered by fair hiring laws. You will see a trend in what is legal and what is illegal—essentially, you cannot ask questions that will reveal information that can lead to bias in hiring, but you can ask questions that relate to job performance.

- Affiliations: Do not ask about clubs, social organizations, or union membership; do ask about relevant professional associations.

- Age: Do not ask a candidate's age other than, "if hired," can a candidate produce proof that he or she is 18 years of age.

- Alcohol or Drug Use: The only allowable question relating to current or past drug or alcohol use is, "Do you currently use illegal drugs?"
- Criminal Record: Do not ask if a candidate has been arrested; you may

ask if the candidate has ever been convicted of a crime.
- Culture/Natural Origin: You may ask if the individual can, "upon hire," provide proof of legal right to work in the United States. You may ask about language fluency if it is relevant to job performance.
- Disability: You may ask if candidates can perform essential job functions, with or without reasonable accommodation; and you may ask them to demonstrate how they would perform a job-related function. You may ask about prior attendance records. And you may require candidates to undergo a medical exam after an offer of employment has been made.

- Marital/Family Status: Questions about marital status and family issues are discouraged except as they relate

to job performance, as in the child care example above.
- Personal: Avoid questions related to appearance, home ownership, and personal financial situation.
- Race/Color: No race-related questions are legal.
- Religion: If Saturday or Sunday is a required work day, you may ask candidates if they will have a problem working on those days.
- Sex: You may ask if a candidate has ever worked under another name. Be sure not to make gender-related assumptions about job capabilities.

How to Deal with Information that is Volunteered

Despite your careful preparation and question selection, some candidates will volunteer information that you would prefer not to know. The best way to handle this situation is not to pursue it nor to make note of it. You can't erase the information from your memory, but you can eliminate it as a discussion point and selection factor.

Consistency Equals Fairness

Carefully planned questions and a structured interview process that is the same for all candidates will ensure equal treatment of all who apply. Keep the focus on what the job requires and how each candidate has performed in the past. Perhaps most importantly, make fair hiring part of your company's mission and value statement, championed from the top down and an integral part of the selection process.

Additional Suggested Questions

· Tell me about yourself.
· Why are you interested in this position?
. What are the most significant accomplishments in your career?

- Describe a situation in which your work was criticized.
- What do you know about our organization?
- How would you describe your personality?
- How do you perform under pressure?
- What have you done to improve yourself over the past year?
- What did you like least about your last position?
- Are you leaving (did you leave) your present (last) company?
- What is your ideal working environment?
- How would your co-workers describe you?
- What do you think of your boss?
- Have you ever fired anyone?
- What was the situation and how did you handle it?
- Are you creative?
- What are your goals in your career?
- Where do you see yourself in two years?
- Why should we hire you?
- What kind of salary are you looking for?
- What other types of jobs/companies are you considering?

www.ingramcontent.com/pod-product-compliance
Lightning Source LLC
Chambersburg PA
CBHW070956220526
45471CB00007B/3059